Living Single the Right Way

Living Single the Right Way

Betty J. Gibbs

ISBN: 978-1-957724-16-4 (Paperback Edition)
ISBN: 978-1-957724-15-7 (Hardcover Edition)
ISBN: 978-1-957724-17-1 (E-book Edition)

Book Ordering Information

The Regency Publishers, US
521 5th Ave 17th floor NY, NY10175
Phone Number: (315)537-3088 ext 1007
Email: info@theregencypublishers.com
www.theregencypublishers.com

Printed in the United States of America

DEDICATION

I dedicate this book to young people everywhere. You are the present and our future.

Individuals need to know who they are, and how to not only survive life, but to live it. In order to do this, they must be able to recognize life's issues, and know how to deal with them. I aspire my book to be a tool in achieving this purpose.

Acknowledgments

First, I give thanks to my children Demarcus, Shacoria, and Adina for their constant pushing me to complete this book. There were many obstacles, but you always encouraged me.

I also give thanks to Pastors, Apostle Carl Franklin, and Pastor Hattie Franklin. Your prayers and support rescued me in my storms. Restoration by you empowered me with unfolding abilities to write this book.

I thank (the late) Paula Flournoy of the Fountain of Life Kingdom Center, and Ann Burton at the Broadmoor Middle Laboratory School. Your input made such an extraordinary impact, regarding my writing this book.

Lastly, if it were not for the millions of individuals needing direction out of their state of darkness, there would be no need for people like me or this book. I am just one of thousands, who are committed to helping others in need.

Ultimately, all thanks and glory be to God.

Contents

INTRODUCTION

Living Single

Single is a quantitative word, which refers to only one whole person or thing. In reference to one's social status, it refers to an unmarried individual. However, according to concordances in the bible, there are absolutely no word listings of the term "single". So, how do we find out what's right, according to God's perspective of "living single"?

I will make an attempt to lay down the basics of "living single the right way". It is the way God intends for us to live as individuals. Though no man knows the mind of God, He does give us divine revelation, by the leading of His Holy Spirit.

If we can stop judging each other long enough, we will realize that our experiences make us who we are. However, various persuasions can change us for better or worse. We look upon people, but we don't know their story. This book addresses the pieces of the story little by little, until the story as a whole can be understood. We don't need to know anyone's whole story. But, if we could just understand where they are coming from, life can be so much easier.

Like putting on 3D glasses to see things from a 3D perspective, I will attempt to give a few biblical pointers up front. This will help to understand God's way from a believer's perspective. Also, we can learn how to benefit from the things of God, when seeking His help.

The Bible

Consider the bible as a tool of instruction that guides us to righteousness, which is the right way of life. Who do we trust in our lives more than anyone? Is it our parents, a love one, our job or boss, our teacher or mentor, friend, ourselves or spouse? If God is not our most trustworthy friend, then we are in trouble! That which comes out of the womb is limited in time. God is infinite, and sits in eternity.

Time is expressed in units of periods, but eternity is the end of all time. If a man lives to be a thousand years, his experiences, knowledge, or wisdom could not come close to the knowledge of God. Why trust a job, car, or circumstance more than we trust Almighty God? God used His own creation to write about who He is, by demonstrating what He does, done, and will do. Who are we to question the Bible, which is His autobiography (Books of Law)? We were not born with the knowledge we possess now, no matter what title or degree we have. Our knowledge was obtained by experiences, things, family, and people who have crossed our paths.

However, God is timeless! The bible says that God is "…the Alpha and the Omega, the Beginning and the End" (Revelation 21:6). These two periods are represented by Greek symbols. They are too great in number to be included in our daily time systems. We can't envision either of these, on a clock or calendar. Look at the numbers 0-9, which we can see and measure. They are so much lesser than God's beginning (Alpha); and therefore, could not come anywhere close to his end (Omega)! He's just that AWESOME! And, He is too big to be seen with the naked eye. He has to be in spirit form to show and prove HIMSELF to us!

Believers and Unbelievers

According to the Bible, there are only "believers" and unbelievers". There's no such thing as a nonbeliever, because everything and everyone know that God exist. Unbelievers know God, and choose not to believe, or have anything to do with Him. They don't want to know the word that God has spoken, what He does for others, or how He makes miracles happen. They just don't want to know Him, and they prosper in their own ways.

Believers, on the other hand, know and accept that there is a true and living God. However, there are two types of believers committed and uncommitted believers.

Committed Believer

A committed believer knows God, and has made a decision to live for Him. Their nature is to learn about the things of God. They reverence God, in both the physical and spiritual realms. Some examples are going to church, serving, worshiping, fasting, praying, and praising God. Another way is by taking on the personality (nature) of Jesus Christ, the Son of God, to demonstrate the character, will, purpose, and plan of God.

Uncommitted Believer

An uncommitted believer knows that God exists, but they have no personal relationship with Him. It's like having knowledge of a celebrity or song artist, but not knowing them personally. To connect with them we just simply buy their DVD or CD, and blog, Facebook, twitter, email, or write to them. An uncommitted believer goes through other believers to connect to God. This is done, instead of going to Him directly, because they have no personal relationship with Him. They try praying and asking God for things, but are unsure of the process. They also lack the faith, or confidence needed to get the blessing they seek.

On the other hand, some are bold and believe that they are in right standing with God. They are drinkers, smokers, adulterers, fighters, talebearers, deceivers, thieves, murderers, and etc. Like the unbeliever, they depend on themselves, others, and their own resources to meet their needs.

Fortunately, God is just and faithful to everyone, whether believer or unbeliever, committed or uncommitted.   His mercy and His grace are given to all men. God desires that every man should live, and not perish, but have everlasting life (John 3:16).

God's Will and Purpose

What is God's will, and God's purpose? We hear that a lot in life, but what are they exactly? One's will is one's choice, consent, or desired way to act upon something. God's will is the chosen way, He intends for His plan to be carried out. This is the righteous way or state. He wants us to be in a state of righteousness while living. The bible shows what has happened throughout history, when man's choice, consent, or desire is to obey or disobey God (His will).

God's purpose is the reason, why we do what He has commanded or ordained us to do. In a nutshell: God has a righteous way (His will) for us to execute His plan, so we can accomplish His purpose and our purpose, which is our destiny!

CHAPTER 1

KNOW YOURSELF

Living single the right way entails getting our lives aligned with the word of God. We must first know everything about the essence of our own lives. It is not just good enough to know that we have some issues. Make note of what they are. Why? The reason is that we need to deal with them. Don't just say to someone, "Yeah, I know I've got issues." We've got to work on correcting them. Nobody wants a package full of holes.

Sometimes, there are things within us that are inherently bad; we are in self-denial about them. Stop denying who we are! Get over it! Just accept it! The sooner we can accept the fact that there are some "not so good things" about who we are, the sooner we can work on them.

How do we find out, who we really are? People can help, if we are not sure. They will say, "He's so controlling!" "She's full of herself." "She's just jealous!" If only a few people are saying this, maybe they are the ones who are envious or jealous. If everyone is saying the same thing, perhaps they are right (most of the time, not all the time)!

DIFFERENT ROLE RESPONSIBILITIES

Know exactly what we are doing with ourselves. It seems like there is no way possible to know our purpose, but I will tell you how. Examine what roles are in our lives (a single student, brother, dad, mom, lady, or sister, etc.). There may be many roles. I am a daughter, sister, cousin, mom, aunt, co-worker, friend, and a Christian. I mentioned all these roles, because there are ties and responsibilities that go along with each.

If we cannot definitively define each role we have, then maybe, we have spread ourselves too thin. Maybe those roles are not significant enough for us to acclaim. For instance; if we don't value being a cousin to our cousins, then by our own convictions, they are simply not worth being a cousin to. It could be that their lifestyles are not up to common standards. Some of us may have relatives that are thieves, gangsters, alcoholics, abusers, users, killers, and other unfavorable characters. In this case, we should pray for them, and love them at a distance. Leave whatever or whomever we can't fix to God.

FIND AND KNOW YOUR PURPOSE

Be "responsible to" the people who are in our lives. THIS IS OUR PURPOSE!!! The Golden Rule in life is to "Do unto others what you would have them to do unto you" (Matthew 7:12). Do not be "responsible for" the people in our lives. But, let's commit to "responding to" whom God has entrusted to us. This does not mean that everyone we meet we owe them valuable time. It's those individuals, whose roles are ordinarily significant, like our family, spouse, and friends that we should give time to. There may be others, but God will lead us to become whatever or whomever He wants us to be to them.

When we know our purpose, we can decide what each goal is for the roles we have. Goals can occur naturally or thought provoking, and set with a planned purpose. For example, the goal of my single mom role right now is to have more organization and order in my household. On the other hand, the goal of my Christian role requires me to have a steady prayer life that exercises the power of speaking things into existence.

We can be or become anyone we choose. Just make sure that we handle those around us, with the proper respect.   It is the people whom God surrounds us with that are instrumental in helping us, to become who we are destined to be. Keep in mind that everyone around us may not be whom God has placed in our lives. Be prayerful, and stick with positive people. If we find only one positive person then hang in there with that one somebody, until God sends someone else.   If there are no positive figures around you, stay to yourself and pray. God will send someone to find you!

ALONE TIME

There are times we can't find anybody to be with. God is like, throwing rocks at our window saying, "Hey! Look up here! I'll help you. Just call me." We call a beautician to fix our hair, and the mechanic to fix our car. Why not call God to fix our bodies, hearts, and souls? You see - even God knows we have issues that need fixing.

He tries to offer help, but we rarely take His advice or help. We call on friends, lovers, sisters, brothers, parents, and grandparents. He's often the last on our list to call for help. It is commonly said, "God help those, who help themselves." Sounds cute, but it's not anywhere in the bible! If we realize we need change, and desire change, God will help us. Think about it. If we can really help ourselves, what do we need Him for?

TESTIMONIAL

I had an alone experience, while carrying my first child. Months before college graduation, one of my classmates started pursuing me. He was not my type, but he kept trying to get my attention during class. I didn't like the distractions. However, I was still alone and very emotional, as a young pregnant student. About 2 to 3 months after his pursuit, we started going out to eat, studying, and spending time together. He visited me, even after graduation. After the birth of my child, we then became intimate. My hormones were out-of-whack, and I was anticipating more attention from him. Well, that didn't happen.

After the second intimate encounter, I accidently found out where he lived. My brother and I were visiting a friend's house. I recognized my friend's car next door then paid him a visit. His wife answered the door with his daughter beside her. I played it off of course: asking if he had a book, for the class we shared. His wife called him to the door. He asked how I was, and what did I need. I continued on about a book for class. He responded that he didn't have it. From that moment on, I was determined not to be with him anymore! I went back to my apartment, and cried to God. I asked God, "Why did you let him treat me like that? I've been talking to you for months about that man!" God said, "You yelled and complained about him all the time. You never once asked for my help."

I was so heartbroken; I could not even go to sleep. So, I repented to God, and asked Him to heal my heart. God did it instantly. I was sleep in less than 5 minutes.

Once we accept who we are, and work on fixing things, we can be true to ourselves. We will then see who we really are, and know exactly what we have to offer.

Issues

I have seen women, on television shows, speak on how hard it is for them to find a man. They make it no secret that they have serious issues. Those issues they have are like outstanding warrants that keep them in jail emotionally. We can't get out of an emotional jail, until we have served reasonable time, working on the issues that got us in there.

Simply, take-up quality time with God, and examine our issues. Then, let Him fix us. It may be hard for some to do, because we don't want to be alone. I have learned that loneliness results from an anticipation of being united with another person. When you're waiting on a mate with expectancy, you are more than likely going to experience loneliness. If you try to just live life (stay busy or focused) during the wait, until it's over, the loneliness will not come. Our alone time is time that God gives us, to be with Him. Even if we give just a little time, not even an hour of our time, God will honor our efforts. Meeting with Him, preferably the same time daily, can and will change our life. Once we spend quality time with Him, we can also get the peace we need. This makes it easier to be who we really are. We don't have to find peace. God will give us peace, and even more of it, when we are doing what He wants and leads us to do.

Straight Talk I

Some people get sick, and do nothing about it. It's okay at times; however, they run the risk of contaminating other people and their lives. Sicknesses (issues) when left untreated, can wreak havoc everywhere. While living life as usual, we do not see the trail of mess we make. At times, we get into multiple relationships thinking we're alright! We don't care about the misery we bring to others, because we are miserable! Stop making a mess of other people lives! Get rid of the issues, and live healthy! Even if the economy doesn't get better anytime soon, we can still live better within ourselves, and in the sanity of our minds. Please understand that this book is about us getting it right with ourselves, regardless if we are dirt poor or filthy rich!

Unresolved Issues

It's hard to maintain a sound or stable life, because of unresolved issues that are too overwhelming. Some of our life's issues are so untamed or multi-facet; they can hinder a normal or naturally good life   For instance, take a female who has large breasts that get in the way of everything she does. The size of her breasts is so huge; it hurts her back, and makes it difficult to walk. Men won't look at her face, without first staring at them. Her clothes fit so awkward; it's difficult for her to wear something, and simply look good in it. Ultimately, the issue with breasts that huge might warrant a breast reduction operation.

I am not advocating such a process, but instead, demonstrating how multi-facet an issue can be. The above statements describe physical issues. However, there are non-physical issues that are spiritual, and may be either emotional or mental. Let me describe to you how a spiritual issue can be just as multi-facet as the physical issue described above.

TESTIMONIAL

I can remember a time when I had severe trust issues, and betrayal going on. Once, a friend I had for 10 years betrayed me in 1 day. I haven't seen her since. She called and told me that she and her sister wanted to take me job hunting. I had just had my first baby, and was looking for a more permanent job than my substitute teacher's job. After coming over to the "housing project" I lived in, she whispered to her sister, "Tell her that we have somewhere else to go." They cancelled out going, where they had inspired me to go. I wasn't sure why.   I sensed she had a problem with what I had become. I was living in the hood with a child, alone without much assistance. They excused themselves that day, and I have not seen her since. I learned that we must be very cautious about "seasonal friends". They can become your worst nightmare, considering all that you have confided and invested in them.

Another betrayal took me down, and only Jesus could bring me up. One night around midnight, there was a knock at my door. When I looked through the peephole of the door, it was an old boyfriend, whom I had loved for some years. I opened the door, because I thought something bad had happened. I let him in. It had been a year and a half, since I last saw him. Now he was in my apartment, and obviously intoxicated. Next, he tried to get him "some". He and I fought a while. Finally, he won. After everything was over, he fell asleep. I was so hurt. Reflecting back, at the end of our pre-existing relationship, we had considered getting married.

The betrayals I had faced, within those last two months, were more than what I could handle. Other betrayals happened as well, around that same time. So I got up, ran upstairs to my bathroom, and fell to the floor. I had (what felt like) a long gash down my back, and blood seem to be leaking everywhere. That was the result of being stabbed in the back (emotionally) multiple times. I felt I was lying in a puddle of blood on the floor. My upper body area was drenched. I felt I was dying. There was no one around to help me. I remembered that my pastor used to pray around three o'clock in the morning. I asked God to tell her to pray for me. Then, I thought, "Maybe she's not up yet". So, I asked God to tell Jesus to pray for me. Instantly, I felt something like a beam of light go straight through me! It healed the gash that was down my back: from the top of my back down to the end of my spinal area. As I got off the bathroom floor, the puddle of blood was no longer there. I was strengthened like never before. I rose up, went downstairs, got a knife, and made my ex-boyfriend get up, and get out!

I heard a man of God say, "You give people RESPECT, but TRUST they've got to earn it." How many times have you trusted someone, and was drugged-up, beat-up, sexually assaulted, stabbed, shot, misused, or mishandled. I stopped putting my trust into people, who didn't know me, or couldn't respect all of me.

We have trusted people with our money, and they have taken it; with our time, and they have mishandled it, and caused it to be wasted; with our emotions, and they have stepped on and injured them; with our minds, and they have confused, abused and torn them down; with our hearts, and they have broken, or ripped it into pieces; with our lives, and they have abused, indecently mishandled and almost killed us; and with things we have acquired, they have stolen, misused, and destroyed them.

Multi-facet issues whether physical or spiritual have to be resolved, before we can live naturally, sound, healthy lives. Remember, God has answers to them all.

CHAPTER 2

FRIENDS

God told me that we should have expectations of our friends. Do you know anyone who calls you, only when they need something? However, they can never give you encouragement, wise advice, a good plan, a way out of something, compassion, money, their time, or anything. Their up days are when they have more than enough to do as they please, and it doesn't include you. Get away from people like this! If they are family members, try to love them from a distance. You cannot be anything other than a wreck and miserable, after lacking what others have taken from you. Giving your all to have someone's friendship is hard work, and it sucks!

The word friend has a precious meaning to it. It should be used only when you know the person well enough to consider them to be your pal, acquaintance, buddy, confidant, or companion. A true friend is constant and unchangeable, in and out of seasons. No one should wear the title of a friend; unless, the two of you can be there for each other. Don't get me wrong. It should never be a favor-for-favor system. That is definitely not being a friend, but a gamester. Be cautious of that game. You'll lose more than what you can afford!

I have learned through experiences that there are seasonal friends, as well. They are what you need for the moment, to get to the next season in your life. A seasonal change (ordained by God) is experienced when everything changes within your environment, for the better. Keep seasonal friends, until life's moment starts to get too awkward. It's when you know that you've grown way pass that point, they are willing to allow you to grow. They will either try to hold you back, or just simply leave you. Let Them Go! You can't move into your new season trying to please them, or other people from your past.

You only need one good friend to have a healthy social life. If you feel you need lots of friends to validate who you are, you should try hard to love yourself. Be a giving friend to yourself first. People you label "friend" can be loud, talkative, and a gossiper: lacking self-control. Let them go, if they are causing too much pain or trouble. This type of so called "friend" is full of drama: overwhelmed with issues that they have not faced or acknowledged! This same individual is also not ready to be a friend, until she or he can earnestly love themselves. It's easy to hate others, when you hate yourself.

Even as children we have issues that can hinder us, from finding or being a true friend. How many times have we heard, "You're not my friend anymore"? The family life we evolve from determines our ability to be or not to be a friend. The values that we are taught or not taught will mold our character. We don't have control over it as a little child. However as we grow older and mature, we can make healthy decisions to change bad qualities and behaviors we have.

A true friend also means accepting each other, despite some of the ongoing issues. Keep in mind, these issues are those that you know you can tolerate. Having patience to help each other mature can be time consuming and trying. It can be worth it in the long-run! When we make conscious effort to get to know ourselves, then we can clearly become a friend to someone else.

FEMALES AND STRANGERS

Be mindful ladies, I want to put something on your mind about the strangers we meet. If you pass by a stranger, speak, and make a little eye contact. Do not feel compelled to give them your number. I am only mentioning this, because some of us are too nice. Men will often stare wittingly with a smile, if he thinks he can get your phone number. Do not give out your number to any or everyone! They will ask for it. Don't do it!

On the other hand, a gamester will come with lines of flattery. "Girl you so fine; you fine as wine." He will make us laugh. He may even boost our self-esteem, but we do not need his lies, drama, or games to make us feel like a star or queen. Believe me - it's only temporary!

Ladies, a gamester always uses oil on you. I don't mean baby or body oil, but dirty oil. He's always trying to be slick: sliding in your life, into your cars, homes, bedrooms, panties, or significant other places. He doesn't respect you, or anything about you! He's all about winning the game (the hunting game).

A real man does not use nasty oil that gets his hands dirty. He's fresh and clean like Clorox: looks clean, smells clean, and is clean. Most of all, he gets rid of the dirt in your life that other men leave behind.

Oh! Don't let me forget one of the most popular players of men - the pimp! He reads foreheads, body language, mood frequencies, dress codes, transportation, or lack thereof, and everything! He takes note of all that you do and don't have. You don't have a man or car (just a hoopty), no money, rundown shoes, jacked-up hair weave, hung-down head, and mismatched clothes. He sees you wanting and hoping someone would love you. It's hard to get rid of him, because he knows he will profit, from all your misfortune.

When females lack love in their lives, and have gone through or put up with so much, we become lost or misplaced. It shows, whether or not we realize it. People, not just a pimp, can see it a mile away. It's written all over us! We are the only ones who don't know it.

TESTIMONIAL

I remember being assaulted by a man once. I called and spoke to my pastor about it. At that time, I had a female pastor. She told me something that really stuck with me. She said, "Betty look at how little my daughter is. Honey you couldn't pay someone to approach or attack her like that." She was right! Her daughter weighed about 85 to 95 pounds. She looked as if someone were to attack her, she would make mincemeat of them. I was 115 pounds at that time. The pastor told me that I should not walk around with my head down, looking as if I couldn't find love.

At first, I thought to myself that her daughter is surrounded by her and her grandmother. They were great teachers and strong black women, who were once activists, in the black community. In my mind, her daughter had so much more support, than I ever had in my family. My mother wasn't a teacher at all, only a provider. Nevertheless, I took heed.

After getting off the phone, I began to say to God, "Lord take everything off my forehead that would make me fall victim to anyone." I started walking with my head up. My self-esteem began to improve. Although, I still didn't have anyone in particular to love me, and it didn't even matter. I started loving myself, and gained a lot of confidence, which I didn't have before. I stopped waiting for love to happen to me, and made it happened for me!

My issues were more about how I had perceived myself, and the fact that I never had a lot of family support or a daddy. Although my family is good, we haven't always shown a lot of love and support towards each other.

STRAIGHT TALK II

Ladies, lose the concept of having a **"piece of a mind."** We should never want a piece of anything, if we can have all of it! Have we heard of wearing a piece of a dress, renting a piece of a house, or driving a piece of a car? This doesn't even sound right! Why would anyone want a piece of a man? Having a piece of a man IS NOT better than having none at all! NO!

Let's get a whole man that's solid. He's not broken like a piece of sidewalk: we have to jump from one fraction of a piece to another, to get to where we're going. This is what he does, with the piece of us he has. He is not faithful. Like the broken yellow street lines on a highway, he keeps crossing over, and going into other lanes (relationships). That straight, solid, gold line should not be crossed over, except in certain instances.

Settling for a piece of a man is actually having a **"piece of a mind."** We need a whole (sound) mind to function properly! We can't think right, trying to figure out how to keep a piece of something that's not ours. We're too busy running toward, and stalking a piece of rock that we think is a piece of gold! Let's get rid of this foolishness!!!

GOOD SINGLE MEN

To all you good single men, "**Beware of broken glass**". It starts out a full bottle, which becomes empty, and is thrown into trash heaps. That's what makes it broken, and of no use. Females, who are hurt (broken, full of issues) and not trying to get help, have become broken glass. At times, they seem to fall into the hands of good men.

These men become mesmerized by the "**shine**" of the broken glass, which is all that's left, of what they once were. This glass will cut up your heart, money, house, and cars: practically all your possessions! Everything it touches is ripped to shreds! The men may end up damaged goods, and incapable of being anything to anyone – sometimes scarred for life.

One of the worse mistakes is to shack-up with them. More damage is done, because babies can result, from the long-term or even short-term union of the two.

Set desired standards for what you want or desire in a woman. Beauty and drama can be found or seen everyday on television. You want a lady whose lifestyle shows evidence of those standards, and are visible by all who knows her.

Scout around for diamonds. They are worth sharing everything with, and go well with every precious thing you do. There is so much more you can do with something that's special: no matter where you go.

Can you imagine taking diamonds out to eat with you? Everyone will notice you. How about walking in the mall or anywhere? Look at all those who are in awe of you! Imagine having diamonds in the bedroom. They will actually light up every room in the house! Wow! What a feeling! What a woman! What a life! Keep in mind, real diamonds cut glass. Get rid of the broken glass that's Tearing Up Your Life!

Straight Talk III

Make sure that you good men are good like you think you are. There are good men who smoke, drink, and sell drugs. They are entrepreneur minded, blue-collar, white-collar, but controlling, and a few other opposing-in-nature attributes. Get rid of your bad habits, so you'll be polished along with her. You may seem to be the best of the trade. Make sure you are up to part on being "**THE M-AN**". Do you want diamonds? The man that should have them should be someone who's strong enough, mature enough, or prosperous enough to get them, and maintain their up-keeping. It takes a real man to know how to do this.

Roommates

To those who are single and live alone be careful, when letting other people stay with you. I didn't say, "Don't help anyone." However, be very careful with roommates. You yourself are already single, and have some issues – no doubt. If someone else moves in, you'll have to be strong enough to deal with your own issues, and the other person's as well. Very few young people can do this, whether effectively or not.

Moving a friend in can not only be discomforting, but regretful, and dangerous at times. The friend may be having financial or parental problems. Even when you think it's no big deal - it is. Really, it is! The lack of someone having sufficient money, for themselves, will lead to them borrowing or stealing from you. You'll go out, but wait until you get back. They'll have on your clothes, or have eaten something you bought, just for you. They may invite company that they have never discussed with you.

If the friend is co-dependent on you, because of parental problems, they may do drugs or alcohol. If it's the parents of the roommate that do the drugs or commit abuse, you are still left with a fight on your hands. You will have to try stabilizing your friend's emotions, once they start living with you. This is a job!

Emotional issues are often times deep with un-forgiveness, nightmares, irritability, rage, depression, worrying, crying spells, shouting moods, obsessive eating habit, extensive weight loss or gain, promiscuity, and self-hate. I'm just saying! If you are socially single, leave the "taking people in" to older families. Older families will have the wisdom and patience to deal with someone's issues. They can work on helping them too.

However, if you chose to roommate with a friend that's stable and of a sound mind, still be careful! Let me tell you what I told my children, about picking their friends. I told them, "When you choose a friend, make sure that friend has issues you can deal with." I advised my daughter. "If your friend hates how good you look in an out-fit, and how long your hair is, stop laughing and ignoring her. She could set you up, when given the opportunity!" I have seen girls set up other girls to get beaten, raped, robbed, and even killed. It was because the girl disliked a lot about the one she calls "**my friend**". If you've got haters, keep them at a distant, and not in your house!

I admonished my son as well. "If you hang-out in class with a guy, because the two of you clown in school, be careful. It may be that when he leaves school, he likes to rob old people, and take people purses or cars. You had better leave him in the classroom. Don't bring him home with you! That young man may think what he does is funny, because he has no values, or conscious about it." These are the people you need to always observe, and keep at a distance.

You can't trust even the ones, who come to your parents' house, and call you **"just to hang-out"**. They want you to take a ride with them. Leave them alone! They are only trying to get something from you! It could be your power to do you. This simply means: they will try to change you, your habits, mannerisms, and the way you think. There is something in you they like, or wish they had. Be cautious! Work and get your own car!

STRAIGHT TALK IV

Beware of friends, who've "got game". If you are one with game, and hangout with others that **"got game"**, make sure you're all playing the same game. You might want to beat someone up, from time to time. The other person might want to kill, from time to time. You should get to know the limits of the people you get involved with, before you become friends or start hanging with. Many young people become an accessory to crimes, they didn't know they were a part of.

Please know that someone, whose "got game" will eventually out-smart himself, and risk getting himself killed, or someone else. It doesn't matter whether male or female, they die younger and younger every day. We should find ourselves! Get a handle on these issues, and find God - no matter what!

GOING OUT OF TOWN?

Don't leave town or try to start over, if we have issues, and never figured out what to do with them, or how to solve them. Our issues are obstacles: like rocks we have been hauling around for a long time. If we don't attempt to minimize, or get rid of the rocks we're carrying, we will hit (hurt) other people with them.

Some of those rocks will feel like a ton of bricks. What's so unfortunate is that the people we meet will most likely have their own load of rocks to throw back at us. People with trouble have a tendency to attract trouble.

There is another way to look at going out town with issues. It's like starting a fire in our home town, not putting it out, and going out of town somewhere else to start another one. WHEN DOES IT STOP? It can be suicidal to keep carrying issues around with us, and not solving them. Someone may come along, and pour fuel onto our flames! Let's get ourselves fixed before leaving home! With God's help, find out what our hang-ups are, and try getting rid of them. This helps you keep your sanity, and even your life!

Cry out to God. Tell Him, "I need help! I don't know my purpose in life. Why am I here? Show me! Direct my footsteps, so I can find out what you want, from me."

CHAPTER 3

EIGHTEEN YEARS OLD

Once we reach age 18, we are considered grown, or an adult. The way I see it is: age 18 is the first year of the adult stage in life. The law imposes upon 18 year olds to know what accountability is. Ironically, many teens at this age are trying to prolong their childhood, or rush into full adulthood.

I think that an 18 year old starts to transition into an adult at 13 years old, but it can become an extended growth phase. It should be based on what they've been taught and learned. If a child has little to no teaching about responsibilities, and life itself (how to cook, wash clothes, grooming techniques, etc.) what exactly are they accountable for at 18?

There are processes that every individual ought to know, prior to becoming an adult. Although it's up to the parents to teach the child, parents sometimes miss the mark (by a long shot).

Here is the problem. Some parents **"expect"** their children to learn certain things on their own. Ironing is a good example. You sometimes expect the child to look at you ironing, and catch on, just like that. However, if you don't say to a child, "Come let me show you how this is done", there is no guarantee that the child was positioned to learn. Was he planning on learning? You don't know. Was he paying attention? You don't know. Did he learn how to iron? You don't know!

The second problem is: you expect a child to **catch on** to a process **by a certain age.** The parent simply has expectations toward the child's ability to learn, without any real form of teaching practices. Stop assuming, and having un-fulfilled expectations, about what your child knows. You have to make sure that you teach the child, and you can be confident that they do know. Although this seems elementary, **"an unlearned child is an unlearned adult".** A lot of issues result from uneducated adolescents: like negligence, abuse, alcohol, drug co-dependencies, unwanted pregnancies, and etc.

On the other hand, an eighteen year old that's mature, and on his/her own has been taught well. He or she knows how to be independent. They will acquire a job, an apartment, condo or house. Positive social interaction will keep them alert, and on beat, with their roles and responsibilities.

However, as mature as they are, they can possibly become over confident. That's not to say that some are mature, get married, and do well in life. However, there are some that may marry too soon, and are not as responsible as they think. This does not sound like a problem to you, but it could be worse than imaginable. An early marriage constitutes shared identity. Young males and females need separate identities, when they initially become adults. Once you share your identity continuously with someone else, in the initial stage of adulthood, you may lose it. "It's never about what **"I want"** any more, but about what **"you or we want."** Does that statement sound familiar? One may start to feel like he or she has lost some things: like the social freedom of wanting to go out, and be with others of their own choosing, or even going out of town with friends.

Another problem is the premature parenting stage which comes within the first 2-3 years of marriage. This will lead a young married couple straight to Heartbreak Hotel. If these conditions do not apply to you, please don't get offended. I won't lie to you! There are some young newlyweds in this predicament who will and have weathered this storm. Fortunately, they have had positive teachings, healthy environments, intervention, and support systems to sustain their marriage.

STRAIGHT TALK V

Now that I know what I know about life, it seems unfair to get married at 18, or have a baby before or at this age. It just seems if we could be an adult for five or more years, do it to enjoy the freedoms of adulthood. Get use to life's responsibilities. Strive to be self-sufficient, before getting into a relationship. Hopefully college is what both male and females pursue at 18. If not, perhaps entrepreneurship (starting a business via internet or home business) may be an option for you as well.

A young man, whether in college, working or not, should be an addition to a female, and not a subtraction. Put time back into her busy schedule, by helping with the small stuff. She shouldn't to try to take time out of her day to pick you up. Go see her! Make sure you are self-sufficient, pain-free, or bearing as little issues as possible. Most ladies, whether independent or not, want a man who can give her something in addition to himself. What can you render to her? You can't sneak and take her somewhere with your uncle's car, mother's money, brother's clothes on, selling cans or metal scrap to afford the movies!! No! Not acceptable! Just be respectful, and tell a female you can't get involved right now. I know it sounds crazy. But, why talk to a female when she has to pay for your hair cut, food, and deodorant; then provide your transportation? Have some dignity about yourself. Tell her now is not a good time for you. If the two of you are meant to be together, God will make it happen. Make sure you are ripe, before starting anything. You know - get a place of your own, a vehicle to drive, and a job for money.

A young female whether in college, working or not, should definitely strive for self-sufficiency. More is expected of you: how you keep your body, how many guys you are intimate with, if you're pregnant or not (if so, will abortion be pursued), and a myriad of social concerns pertaining to being a young female. Males are looking for girls to be intimate with, and some maybe searching for marriage even. There are many games awaiting you, from both males and other females. Be a friend who can advise, encourage and make strong. Don't get caught up having fun, sitting up gossiping, being drama plagued, or playing sex games. Make sure you are confident, in who you are and what you want. You don't want to fall victim to anyone, because you have needs and seeking provision.

Plan not to struggle! How we start as an adult does not necessarily mean that's how we will end up later. Change can happen either intentionally or un-expectantly, for better or worse. It can render a different outcome at any time, in our lives.

Teenage Parenting

As a teenager, it's very hard to be subject to parenthood. One will be torn between wanting to go out, and party, verses staying at home and being a mom or dad to a baby. Early parenting is a ball of bondage to a young teenager's social freedom.

I'm very grateful that my firstborn didn't happen until I was 23 years old. This gave me five years to get a college education, meet other people, go out and have fun. I went out to the skating rinks, bowling alleys, on dance floors, at the shopping malls, and out-of-town visits.

Social fun is the difference to having a healthy adolescence or a dysfunctional one. When one has to choose from being a stay at home parent, or a very sociable and popular teen, there are no comparisons.

Teenage parenthood can be very scary and dangerous. Most teens are without family support, or have very little, if any. Emotions of wanting to be a child are still surfacing after parenthood. You are torn. Although circumstances prove you to be a grown adult, your developmental stage is still that of a teenager or young adult.

The thought of not being able to go out and socialize puts the baby at risk of being unwanted. An unwanted baby sometimes will suffer abuse and neglect. The parent, on the other hand, suffers depression, loneliness, family pressure, peer pressure, confusion, and other derogatory emotions.

If you find yourself at a place like this, stop and get help from someone! An older adult is preferred. They already have a family, and can steer you in the right direction. People your age seldom have the knowledge or wisdom you need to get the help you're seeking. They may be able to relate to you, but often can't lead you out of the woods. If you are desperate, go straight to God. Sometimes, a relationship with the baby-daddy, baby grandparents, and your parents can all be so confusing.

Keep in mind, one still have issues to sort out and eliminate with the added responsibility of parenthood. This can be so overbearing. However, "God promised to put no more on you than you can bear" (I Corinthians 10:13). But, the Devil didn't promise he wouldn't. So, make sure you pray! If you don't know how to pray, read the "Our Father Prayer" (in the New Testament book of Matthew 6: 9-13), as often as you need.

YOUNG MEN

I have a message to the young men. "Please put a value on who you really are, and find your purpose!" Men are natural predators, and great observers. However, it's what you see other men do that will sometimes influence, or determine what you do. You either want to do what they do, learn from them, or just deposit into your mind what others do for later comparisons.

In my opinion, I always thought if I show my son how to be responsible then I could teach him how to be a man. Here's a fact; people learn by hearing, seeing, touching (hands-on) tasting, and smelling. Different people learn by ways of these five senses. Though my son can hear and see how I handle responsibilities, it's not enough. He is still in search of a man's hands-on method, which is proven the most effective way of learning for him. I keep showing him stuff, but it's not making the impact that I hope for. A woman does not handle things like a man does, and vice versa. I bet most men would say, "You can't send a woman in to do a man's job." That's the bottom line! And, I agree whole-heartedly! So after **"all I think"** and have taught him, he still seeks the guidance and counsel of a man. He has much gratitude and respect towards me as his mom, while seeking his father's affirmation.

STRAIGHT TALK VI

When young men (who have gone to jail) get interviewed, they often say that they didn't know their father. However, there are young men who are successful from single parent homes. They were influenced by their mother, and others as well. The mother was strong and responsible. She had both good survival and living skills. That means she was both a provider and a teacher.

I am persuaded to believe that boys, who really need men figures as role models in order to become successful, are those that come from generations lacking strong and wise male figures. If there was no father, but an uncle, older cousin, or nephew, then there's your role model. It is not just the absence of a father in the immediate family which stunts a boy's manhood. It's the lack of strong men in the surviving generations as a whole. Grandma didn't have a male strong enough to stand up to the plate. Auntie didn't have a real man. Mama didn't bring home a man to help him become a real man.

YOUR LIFE IS A SEED

When I was young, I remember having a friend, who lived with his mom and stepfather. His stepfather spent a lot of time with him as a child, and taught him many things. My friend really loved his stepfather, because that was the closest male in his life. I remember my friend telling me how his stepfather would get mad at times, and take him to the backyard. While back there, his stepfather advised him to drink hard liquor. The stepfather would tell him, "This is what you do, when people start acting crazy with you. Man just drink you a little something to calm your nerves, and forget about them." Even though my friend had a father figure in his life, a seed of alcohol addiction was planted and deposited, into the growing stages of his life. My friend gradually became an alcoholic, and still is to this day. You want positive people to deposit productive seeds into the growing stages of your life. As you grow, you will have all the important support systems tied into, and functioning inside of your character. Strive to be with positive people. You will get more out of life, and strength to keep it. Negative people will deposit negative seeds that will leave you shipwrecked, imprisoned, on the streets, or in the grave.

Keep in mind that you are a seed in someone else's life, so watch what you sow. The Bible says in the book of Galatians 6:7, "...Whatsoever a man sows that he will also reap".

The way you talk and dress; your mannerisms on how you respond to things; and the type of music you play are some common ways seeds are sown, into the lives of other people. If you never say a word, your body language has said something to someone.

A young man pulled up next to my car at a red light. Loud profane music was playing on the radio or CD. I wanted so badly to yell at him, "Stop sowing those nasty seeds in my spirit!" I didn't want that song lingering in my head. I try to guard my spirit well. Remember that the words you speak will impact somebody's life. Whether or not the intent is good or not, God holds you accountable. The Bible says, "For every idle word men may speak, they will give account of it..." (Matthew 12:36-37).

Make sure what's sown as a young man doesn't make you a barren old man. That's what happens when one sows too many reproductive seeds, out of season! He will have nothing to invest in as he ages; although, he tries diligently.

Eventually marriage will happen, and the lifestyle of a young man will tell off on him. The tool he sows reproductive seeds with will stop functioning well. It is often due to the reckless usage of it. That's how it is with anything! If you don't use it the way the instructions (God's word) tell you to, it will lose its power or ability to function properly. We can't rig-up everything!!! When God made us we were given instructions, "Be fruitful and multiply..."

(Genesis 1:28). It was given to Adam and Eve, because He made them one (married). Therefore, they were free and capable to do what He commanded them.

These instructions were given to married people only, and not to single males or females. Celibacy should always be a single person's coat and hat, or badge of honor. The only one who can strip you of your garment is you, not society, family or peers. Although, someone may take them by force!

CURIOUS, ODD & SINGLE

There are times in our lives we may become a little too curious. This curiosity can lead to a lot of things. We can become too radical about life sometimes. Maybe it stems from too much boredom: not having enough to do socially, physically or mentally. Then, we take away the boundaries, allowing too much immoral and indecent behavior to flood our lifestyles. This is where body piercing, chemical dependencies, parental rebellions, thought transformations, gender changing and opposing nature erupt! The essence of your very being is to be radical, weird, and out of control!

Body piercing and other external changes are messages that the individual no longer likes, who they are. Let's be clear. Everyone who has body piercing, or gender changing or external changes is not necessarily this individual. However, it is when two or more of these traits, with radical behavior are all operating simultaneously. These individuals are not getting the recognition they want; therefore, it becomes a rebellion. The mind-set implies, "If no one pays me any mind, then I'll fix them. I'll be something that no one likes for sure, or I'll get their attention. Somebody is going to notice me before I'm done making a statement."

The reality of all this is hell for the parents of adolescents, who go through this. The minds of these adolescents can be reached! The answer involves going out on a limb to get them; although, they don't seem to want to be rescued. I deliberately used the word "limb", because it's a place that can be very hard to reach, depending on how high it is.

In this situation, being an individual becomes a very alone and isolated person. Family structure is weak or broken, because there is too little positive interactions to combat the isolation. This is analogous to a single healthy atom, which comes into the presence of an infection or virus (negative thoughts and feelings). The infected atom does not remain isolated. It will join other radicals or infected atoms to grow, and take-over more healthy ones. The child will attract, or be attracted by other social radicals, and do more damage. However, there is hope.

The solution is to quarantine the individual socially and emotionally. This is done by taking them way from the infection, and moving them to a different location. Breakdown the radical support system, and replace it with positive family reinforcements. Find a way to bridge family ties: such as going out, if you can afford to. Take visits to the park, as a family, and bring others along. Have family night with television and movies.

Straight Talk VII

All of these things matters to us when we are young, and being molded into an adult. It really matters, if we have issues, and our relatives' issues are far greater or worse than ours. People will say that it doesn't matter what kind of relatives we have; we can do something with our lives. After a certain level of maturity or awareness, it may not matter. But, until we get to that level of maturity or awareness, it does matter. Everything matters, because we are lost until we get there - barely living or surviving.

CHAPTER 4

SUICIDAL & SINGLE (TESTIMONIAL)

I remember being twenty, away from home, and in college. My girlfriends (from high school) talked me into going out of town to college. It was mid-school seasonal break, right after Christmas. I started the New Year away from home. I was introverted. It should not have ever happened. Neither they nor I thought that idea through. My friends were just trying to bring me in on the fun. They were enjoying themselves, because there were no parental authority and rules out of town. It turned out to be a bad idea for me.

Many childhood issues resulted in me being introverted. I was molested from ages 3-5 years. It stopped and resumed, when I reached age 8 in foster care. No one knew what I had gone through, not even my mom. It was childhood pain that became emotional baggage. At this point, it did not matter how the wounds of childhood pain were made. The fact was - it existed.

So there I was, living in a multi-cultural environment, on a college campus. About 260 miles from where I had come from, men of all ethnic groups were pursuing me. Now, this may not have been a big deal to a lot of you, but I was not a player.

As a matter of fact after having been molested, and being the attention of many males I dropped into a severe depression. I was overwhelmed. My mother and family (as a whole) were always my shield of covering. There was no longer any covering, once I moved out of town. I became fearful of what might happen to me. Before ever realizing it, I became suicidal. A deep depression engulfed my life. It was right in the middle of me furthering my education.

It showed up in ways no one would have suspected anything wrong. For instances, I started having the need to be needed by my friends. I counseled and advised them on everything: from clothing fashions to hair, cooking, friendships, and relationships in general. I just could not be left alone for long periods of time. I had visions of tragedies flash before me. I slept only two hours a day for the entire fall semester (including weekends). I studied all night far passed midnight. My dorm room was on third floor. I would always see myself falling, and rolling down 3 flights of stairs, each time I left the dorm building. I had to go to my classes daily, and traveled across a ravine to get to them. I would always see the ravine falling, and my body falling beneath it onto the rocks. Tragic visions flashed before my eyes in everything I did, like something in horror movies.

At the end of the semester, I was the last one to leave my dorm suite. My ride back home was delayed an additional four hours. I had to contact a friend back home to keep from committing suicide. The desire to be home with family had become so overwhelming, I wanted to kill myself, because getting home was not happening fast enough!

After being at home, I started going out dancing 2 to 3 times a week. This was very abnormal for me. Fortunately, my godfather noticed my behavior. He took me to a hospital, and it suggested that I seek counseling. That's exactly what I did.

A friend drove me around town looking for a place of counseling. After driving around for a little while, he asked, "What are you going to these places for"? I told had him that I needed some answers and counseling. He said, "You give me thirty dollars; I'll get my black bible, and counsel you." Then he tells me to go to God. I told him that God wanted me to get counseling. He said to me, "You lying on God!"

So, I told him I would go back to God, and I did. That same weekend I visited a holiness church. The preacher told everyone during prayer time, "Lift your hands up to God. Close your eyes, and tell God what you want." I did exactly that. I asked God, "Please give me back my mind?" Guess what? He did it! The next day, I woke up, and heard birds chirping! I couldn't remember, at any time, not hearing them. That indicated to me my mind had really been set free!

Your expressions of pain may be different than mine; nevertheless, they are real. You can go to God, and He will wipe away, any and all, your pain. This may seem too simple, for some of us to grasp. But, really, that's all it takes. Confess your pain, and ask God to heal you. Like the good father He is, God always wants to make things better for us. Sin may not be the only thing which leads to our hurt. God waits on us to ask for healing and deliverance. He will not force on us what we need!

MARRIED AND SINGLE

There are married individuals living single lives. We know who we are! We went through the motions of getting married, because we like and want the benefits only. Like the uncommitted believer, we boldly act like we are in good standing with our spouses. Our hearts are full of pretense and deception, and God knows it!

When our spouse is at work or school, we are busy living the single life, at the expense of the marriage. We are using money and credit cards like stores are going out of business! We have adulterous relationships, with males or females that really make us want to do more of what we shouldn't be doing.

It becomes hard for the real man and women to get a good and faithful spouse. How? We ship-wreck their lives, by changing the way they love and feel, about everything! Instead of giving and loving freely, now they walk on a tight rope, trying to weigh and balance everything!

Why are we doing this? We've got some unresolved issues that are buried or hidden. We are not even trying to deal with them! We take more pleasure in living a lie, instead of being true to ourselves and others. We just need to repent! Repent to God, our spouses, and ourselves! I am not joking. Confess to God our issues, and why we did what we did. God will forgive us, whether or not our spouse does.

Another scenario of being married and single is when a young lady falls for the "butt-hole of the year". Although, she's fought with him throughout their entire relationship, she still gets pregnant, and marries him. Now married, they are yet feuding and dysfunctional as a family.

There is no being there for each other, because it was always a one-way street from the start. This happens, because a young female can be so traumatized by growing up without real love or a daddy. At some point, she fall's victim to the ultimate player, and cannot rise above the cycle of abuse. The relationship is just sexual and abusive.

That female may go through cycles of abuse, until it almost kills her. She will become isolated due to the lack of a support system, family, and real friends that have somehow been cut off from her. If we know a female like this, pray for her. I am a firm believer that prayer changes things! If we are one of these victims, get away from what is hurting or killing us. Go to God. He cares, and will help us.

DIVORCED AND SINGLE

Too many marriages are resulting to divorce. Divorce constitutes a death experience. Marriage vows end with the words, "...until death do us part". Therefore, the parting in divorcement is a grievous process by which the family institution is killed. Even if divorce is needed like in the case of abuse, the experience of death impacted is still severe and traumatizing.

Marriage ties are bonds that are tied so tight that they are one. Once separated, the individual torn bond must be processed before it can be tied to another one. In other words, after divorce an individual must get fixed!

Many times, a divorced person starts seeking out another lover to help heal their broken heart or life. Typically, all they do is bleed all over someone else's life, because they are bleeding, torn, broken, and raggedy. The body itself is not torn, but the heart is. That's why, we cannot go to anyone before we go to God first. Our hearts are spirit, and spirit cannot be fixed physically, but spiritually by God!

If divorce results from abuse, it's like being the victim of a car collision. Our lives will be severely wrecked. We must go to the hospital! We may sustain head and body trauma. In addition to the mind being discombobulated, there might be severe chest pains, internal injuries and external bleeding, or bruising.

The Throne of Grace is the only hospital that can help us in this situation. Take the children too! They sustain lots of injuries, as well. No one should get out of a severe car wreck and, attempts to be with anyone, while they themselves are half dead. That's preposterous!!! Stop avoiding God! The longer we wait, the longer we will bleed. Our lives will no longer be the same. We may never live again! We might breathe a little, but on a respirator: never living a healthy functional life!

Keep in mind, "We can't blame the other person for everything!" It is necessary to repent to God, for all that we've done wrong. He knows what we did. Tell God to forgive us for everything we've done that wasn't pleasing to Him during our marriage. Then ask God to heal us, and our children's minds, hearts, and souls. Ask Him to make everyone whole. Do it on your knees, if you can. After all, He is the Mighty King of Kings. We can even lay down prostrate before God, and just cry out to Him. I promise you; not only will He heal us, but He will bless us to be whole and confident.

God is a good God! The sooner we and the family are healed, we can expect to live and have fun again. Whether or not we desire to have another marriage partner, life is good just living healthy. Don't let go of God. Keep Him!!! Our life cannot stay healthy without Him! "God promised, "…I will never leave you nor forsake you" (Hebrews 13:5). Although at some point, we may walk away from Him.

HOMOSEXUALITY

Homosexuals are those who have made a choice to express their genders and/or sexuality contrary to what God has chosen for them. This is an issue that has been around since bible history, and is elaborated on in the book of Romans 1:16-32.

Just like any other issue, there is an underlying problem that causes it. Homosexuality can stem from being raped, molested or sexually abused as a child or adolescent. Most commonly, it stems also from the people we love rejecting who we are. The verbal and physical abuses are what's injuring the mind, and causing one to deny, who and what they are. Instead of finding ourselves, we hide, becoming someone different in the same body. Another common cause of homosexuality is hormonal imbalances. Shockingly, hormonal, imbalanaces are passed down from the mother, during the delivery process too. Too little or too many testosterone in the male, and estrogen levels in the female are what produce these imbalances.

Unfortunately, there are even worse things that causes homosexuality – incest. Every child need a mom and dad. However, when mom or dad molests that child, that parent is no longer desired. Depending on the need (various factors), the child may still want to appease that same abusive parent. The irony in all this is - a child with no father or mother desires a parent(s), but the child molested by a parent desires to get away from them.

As a result, the need to transform one's sexuality can sometimes become the defense or coping mechanism.

If one is born with female genitals, that individual is a female. Likewise, if one is born with male genitals, this individual is a male. How one has chosen to display who he/she is an individual's choice. More importantly, God made the choice for us before we ever knew ourselves or was born. God is our maker. Just simply submit to Him, and turn ourselves in. Stop resisting and running from God! It is written, "He that is not with me is against me…" (Luke 11:23). We must be walking in obedience to his word to be with Him. He loves us. Let him give us a make-over. Stop letting man, society, or circumstances make us over!

Deformities happen within the womb of expecting mothers. Factors that cause them may be what the mother takes internally, the environment or atmosphere she lives in, or physical and external encounters that are harmful to the pregnancy and the mother. Despite all this, God can change the outcome! He will put doctors, mentors, or advisors in our pathways to help with those issues. Many times we reject the help, just like we reject God.

Romans 12:1 KJV

"I beseech you therefore brethren, by the mercies of God that you present your bodies a living sacrifice, holy, and acceptable to God, which is your reasonable service."

Romans 12:2 KJV

"And do not be conformed to this world, but be transformed by the renewing of your mind, that you may prove what is that good and acceptable and perfect will of God."

Submit to God. We will become the best that we can be in Him. We have to confess with our mouths from our hearts. We must tell God that we are sorry, for using the body He has given us in an unnatural way. Don't forget to ask for forgiveness, and forgive yourself! God loves us just the way He made us. We stopped loving ourselves, but God didn't stop loving us!

STRAIGHT TALK VIII

Who has the authority to condemn homosexuality? God our maker condemns homosexuality from generation to generation. Don't forget that is why Sodom and Gomorrah were destroyed by fire! So no matter how polished of a lifestyle we make of it, God will not bless that lifestyle, or that of an adulterer, idolater or fornicator - according to I Corinthians 6:9. It does not mean you won't prosper. However, the bible says, "The blessing of the Lord, makes one rich, and he adds no sorrow with it" (Proverbs 10:22). How God blesses us is always greater than what we can do for ourselves, because He's greater than us.

TESTIMONIAL

I was a fornicator (having premarital sex) when I was young. Fortunately, I didn't die while young, because I would have died in my sins.   The old folk used to say, "You would have bust Hell wide open". Progressively, what happened is that I grew up. I got old enough to realize that trying to find a relationship **"my way"** was not worth losing my soul. I was trying to live a Christian life with Jesus, but I kept fornicating. Although, it's common practice socially, God frowns on it!

I kept going to church, because it is important to me to have a relationship with God. Why? Because - God always keeps me alive when circumstances and people try to kill me. As a little girl walking with my sister across town, a German Sheppard dog charged at me. It was right upon my neck. On his hind feet, it was taller than I. At the moment it dashed towards my neck, a stranger caught the dog's collar. The dog was snatched back by the stranger, right before impact. That was God!!!

Also on a cold winter night, sleeping next to an open heater, I was laying on a couch trying to stay warm. A pillow that was under my head caught fire, from the heat coming from the heater. I was on that pillow! The stuffed cushions inside caught fire, and smoke had engulfed the room, and the entire house. Although, nothing had burned, but that pillow!   Everyone was awaken, and got out of the house, without severe smoke inhalation. That was God!!!

When I was in college, and wanted to commit suicide, God kept reasoning with me. He made it difficult for me to take my own life.

These are just a few reasons why being a Christian and serving God is my choice, oppose to living a pleasurable life as a fornicator. I gave it up! I advise you to rethink your choice as a homosexual. Live life the way God intended. It is truly more beneficial giving your life to God than losing it, for the sake of pleasure or your own will. It does not matter who we are, or how good we are to others. God's word does not change nor bend, because it did not bend, nor change for me.

THE SPIRIT OF A PEDOPHILE

Many of us were victimized when we were only a child. The Bible says that "…the devil goes about as a roaring lion seeking whom he may devour" (1Peter 5:8). At the moment you are conceived, the devil seeks ways to destroy you. He has figured out your destiny by your linage. He knows the ancestors we came from, while we don't have a clue. So like a pedophile, he does not discriminate with age. He will victimize a baby or a child, when no one is paying attention. As a result, many of us have been molested, raped, misused, neglected, and abused suffering from

Post Traumatic Syndrome Disorder (PTSD). This is due to past abuse, or attacks from the devil. It may take some people quite a while to understand what I'm saying, but as time pass, a lot of your issues will start making sense. Who we are will also make even more sense.

Those of us who have been victimized by a pedophile spirit will suffer with the inability to trust others. Low self-esteem will have affected our self-worth as we grow. We will walk through life wanting, and looking for someone to love us. It will not happen, until we learn to love ourselves, or God's mercy brings healing into our lives. After thinking very little of ourselves for years, it's not going to be easy. We are not going to know how to give to ourselves, when others have taken so much of us by force!

Not just relationships outside the family are going to be difficult, but within the family as well. It does not matter how old we are now, and what title we possess. If we are still experiencing PTSD (not loving ourselves and having lots of people issues) stop allowing this!

My advice is to look into the mirror that's in your bathroom or bedroom, and tell yourself, "I love you". Keep your head up. Get out of those dark colored clothes, and put on brighter ones. Dark colors have a tendency to keep us depressed, and the joy of a new day suppressed, when we're going through bad times. Start smiling. Let go of your abusive relationships, and grab hold of God's hand. He's waiting to comfort, and heal us of all our past trauma and hurt.

If we have been abused and neglected, there are so many things we just simply have not been taught. Abuse will injure our abilities to learn. Darkness will follow us from one relationship to another, because we will not know how to stop the cycle of abuse.

We must recognize that we are in abuse or been abused, and try to get out of it!

Prayer will be the best way to get away from abuse. Ask God to help us to forgive ourselves for all our unrighteousness, and the others who have wronged us. Tell Him we don't want what we've gone through anymore! We want what He wants for us. Believe it or not, it works! God will hear and forgive us. He will comfort and deliver us, from all hurt and abuse.

Wait on God. He will direct your path. The Bible says, "Commit thy way unto the LORD; trust also in him; and he shall bring it to pass" (Psalms 37:5). This means to give Him whatever it is that we are trying to do. Trust that he can and will perform that that you need, as long it is in His will. Just say, "God I commit this to you". God will do what we may have been trying to do a whole lifetime, in no time. Never assume that God does not hear us. Always try to call on Him. We may not hear Him at first, but when we anticipate an answer from Him, we will get it!

PROMISCUITY AND PROSTITUTION

What are we doing with our bodies? Don't we know that "… our body is a temple of the Holy Spirit" (I Corinthians 6:10)? "… You are not your own" (I Corinthians 6:15). God gave us a will (choice) to do what we choose to do with it. Some of our bodies are into so much debauchery that the holiness of God can't stand to be near us. Because we have chosen to do some nasty things to and with our bodies, disease, tumors, and infections have plagued them. We then wonder what's wrong!

A lot of young men have committed themselves to the beds of females, but not to their hearts. They will schedule everything around being in the bedroom, or shall I say "doo-room" (anywhere the doo is being done). Keep in mind that sex is an **"insatiable"** desire: it cannot be satisfied. According to Hebrews 13:4, "Marriage is honorable in all, and the bed is undefiled".

Men should think back and recognize exactly when did they stop respecting females. Why has the pleasure of sex become more important than the female? Why the DISRESPECT? She's not their wife, but they make her their baby mama - only for the sake of pleasure. They stop caring about her life, with the extension of themselves growing inside of her. These same young men continue seeking sex from other females, and more females. They won't stop hammering inside their bodies, causing cancer and disease to plague someone's sister, mother, cousin, friend, daughter, or wife. If you know someone like that, urge them to stop, and look at what they're doing! They are destroying the lives of young girls, or ladies just for the lack of priority and respect.

Be careful God's word might find us. His laws were written since the beginning of time, and have judged and worked for generations. This simply means that whatever we do will come back to us. Repent to God, and live a healthy, respectful and morally sound life.

Young ladies, lets place more than a monetary value on your body. It should not be used as a bargaining tool for any amount of money. Babies are popping up as symbols of the pleasure we got while having sex.

Most sex is just hardcore, and down right rough. It doesn't sound like anything healthy can result from that! Look at the thrill some get from the pain of tattoos on their body. They are left carrying something around for life like the unwanted child that's conceived in promiscuity. Just as some find ways to camouflage tattoos, so do females as they abort unwanted babies.

The bodies of young ladies can be fragile like a dinner plate. Some dishes are very cheap. We use them, break them, and trash them without any problem! Sometimes we give them away after so much use; we simply don't want them anymore! Men treat promiscuous females, or prostitutes like this. They will use them so much, tear their bodies up from the inside out, and trash them without a problem.

Wake up young ladies! We grant men the access to do this with our bodies! We must treat ourselves respectful like good china that sits in the china cabinet, for special occasions only (preferably marriage ceremonies). Stop being disposable dishes to men! Let's stop washing ourselves off just to be used over and over again! We should save ourselves for special use only (marriage). Give a special man something to touch and feel, in the most precious way known to a man.

If we're having a problem abstaining from intercourse, let's PROTECT OURSELVES. Use condoms and contraceptives. Don't ask God to help us during intercourse! Let's plan not to do it, before we start. We should not place ourselves in vulnerable positions, or places of temptation. Also, we should not allow ourselves to be alone with two or more unrelated (no relationship to us) males at the same time. Be conscious not to wear seductive clothes, in front of a man, intentionally. We cannot allow ourselves to show off everything, thinking no one will take nothing from us. When we expose ourselves, EVERYONE sees us. That's too much accessibility, because most people like to try, get, or buy what they see and like. We have to stop being in denial, and acting unlearned! Someone will eventually take what we're advertising, as a symbol of attraction to play with.

Be observant and wise. Let's stop playing with the super destroyer (sex games). Eventually, we are going to want the marriage commitment, and having a baby to share with our husbands (at some time in life). Please, give him something special to build with.

The tools we utilize to have sex with belong to God, until they are acquired ceremonially (through marriage). This is the only lawful process, by which we have the right to use them. The Bible says, "…do not let any part of your body become an instrument of evil to serve sin" (Romans 6:13). That means no using of the hands, the mouth or tongue to engage in the practice of sin (illicit intercourse)! Oral sex is sex too! It does not matter what type of sex it is. As long as the last name is S-E-X, it's sex!

STRAIGHT TALK IX

There are some rock stars and rappers who have done wrong things with their hands, mouths and tongues on stages, and behind the scenes. However, as they got older, they became fathers and grandfathers, mothers and grandmothers. They grew up, and changed their promiscuous behaviors. Issues and sin exist from generation to generation. Let's grow up! Find God. Get into a relationship with Him. He will protect us from everything that might harm or destroy us!

SINGLE MOTHERS

Conceiving a baby when one is single can be is a mistake most of the time. When Virgin Mary conceived Jesus, she was engaged to Joseph. According to the bible, she was impregnated, by the over shadowing of the Holy Spirit upon her. Although still single, Mary's conception was not through the act of sexual intercourse.   Also, the engagement between her and Joseph was already in progress, prior to their knowledge of God's plan for them. I mention this information with you to demonstrate even while living single a pregnancy isn't always a mistake. God said in His word, "And we know all things work together for good to those who love God, to those who are the called according to His purpose (Romans 8:28)." Mary and Joseph didn't know that God would use their engagement, as a vehicle to bring in "The Messiah". They were willing and "the called".

Sometimes God has allowed pregnancies that have resulted from rape, incest, and molestation to come to fruition, because of His purpose for you and the baby. Both Mary and Joseph had to be visited by an angel to be made of aware of God's planned purpose. We may have been visited by a person whom God has called to stop us from aborting our pregnancies. Yes, having a baby may be turbulent, discomforting or even expensive at times. But, are you a willing vessel (someone God can trust)? Can you trust God?

The act of having the baby, or the baby itself is not a mistake. So, where is the mistake? Well, the first mistake is premarital sex. If one is not married there should be no sexual interactions. The second mistake is unprotected sex. When temptation does present itself, take precautions to avoid premature pregnancies. We all know that it's a risk to jump out of an airplane, but it's reckless to do it without a parachute. Likewise, it's already a sin to have premarital sex, but you don't have to be reckless when you do it.

If God allows a baby to live in the womb 6 to 9 months prior to its birth, then where is the mistake in that? God does not make mistakes! Remember, He still has to add the features, traits, and some things of the parents, before the baby can take form and come forth. Just because we don't see God doing this, it doesn't mean He has no control in the matter. Therefore, when a baby is conceived, God has the power to end the pregnancy at any time!

If He does not abort the baby then why should we? Keep in mind that some of us have yielded our lives to God, and others yield their lives to the devil. The devil makes us think that we are in charge of our own lives. This is a BIG LIE!!! We all know the "Devil is a lie"! We also know that if our breath or heartbeat stops, we have no power within ourselves, to restart either one. See how simple that is! It just goes to show us that we are not Lord over our lives! God is. Imagine some millionaires or billionaires, who may think that their money make them lord over their lives. With all their money power, they can't buy themselves eternal life, and live forever rich!

TESTIMONIAL

In my twenties, I was raped and conceived a child as a result. I didn't report it. I felt if I would just stay away from the culprit, it won't happen again. Two months later, I found out I was pregnant. I was afraid, because the culprit was not only someone I knew, but the spouse of a close friend. I sought the advice from my pastor at that time. The entire incident was handled within the church. It seemed to be the most effective way to resolve it at that time.

I must admit, I didn't want to carry that baby at all. To make matters worse, I was threatened with pre-cancerous cells in my cervix area, and had acquired sexually transmitted infections. I still sought the advice of God and my Pastors. Because of the medical implications, it placed me in a catch-22 scenario. I could abort the baby, or the precancerous cells may spread during my pregnancy, and kill my baby and me. The choice was left solely up to me. Despite my wanting to abort the baby, God had a **"ram in the bush"** answer to my problem.

Let me explain myself. I scheduled to have that abortion to rid me of the shame of being pregnant, and not having a boyfriend. Also, I didn't want to have to explain my stomach being stuck out, while ministering the word of God (outside the church and in the community where I lived). So, on the day I scheduled the appointment to have that abortion, my alarm didn't go off. I did make sure it was set the night before. At the exact time of the appointment, I got a phone call from the Pastor. She told me to turn my television on a certain television channel. There was a talk show on with female guests, who had gone through the exact same medical conditions while pregnant. Each guest had different outcomes. After all was said and done, I decided to continue with my pregnancy. God healed my body, just days before my having the baby, because I would not take my medications properly as prescribed.

Keeping my baby was the best decision I made. After making that decision it was easier for me to breathe, and go on with my life.

SEEKING GOD'S HELP

We must seek God to get fixed! If we could fight the devil by ourselves, why are we so confused, suicidal, or bound? Our issues should not be in existence, if we could get help by staying at home alone. Find the strength, faith, and help of others who know how to resist the devil, and get rid of him!

If you insist on not going to church, stay around the presence of those who show signs that they know the word of God. Keep in mind to read and study the bible for yourself. Reading the word of God will keep you conscious of how you should talk, behave, or fashion yourself, while trying to live righteous. Stay repenting (asking for forgiveness). As long as you keep daily communication with God (reading, meditating and worshiping), He will keep you in perfect peace. The blessings of the Lord will be with you as well.

You cannot pretend to be righteous when going before God. That is deception, and God will know if you are lying to yourself. You cannot lie to Him. He will lead your footsteps, to keep you from going astray. Many can and will lead you astray, if you don't search the truth from God yourself. Ask God for wisdom and knowledge. He will give it to you. Social media can sometimes be a tool of godly things, principles, and word of God. However, "the Holy Spirit… will teach you all things and will remind you of everything he have said to you" (John 14:26).

The Bible tells us "…not to forsake the assembly of the saints" (Hebrews 10:25). When we seek God, don't be side tracked by people, who discourage us from going to church. God will lead us to a good church, where His power and anointing is. He will place us in the pathway of believers, who have overcome our kinds of issues, or know how to overcome them. They will strengthen and encourage us. Even in the movies when someone keeps getting attacked by the same enemy, the individual starts to seek help from people, who know how to fight and win!

Exercise caution. Bad people are everywhere: at school, on the job, in church, at the store, next door, down the streets, on the corner, and everywhere. Keep in mind that others are at the church, and may need more assistance from God than we do.

Go to church. Hear the word of God, and line up what the pastor says with the Bible. Let's not get caught up in doing personal favors with people we do not know. Remember, before we can help someone else, we must first get help for ourselves.

I do not discourage getting counseling. Ask for counseling at church, after attending it several times to check the soundness of what you are hearing. Some things a preacher says may not even sound right. Leave that church, and do not go back! Often times when something feels wrong, do not argue with yourself. Get up, and get out! There are a lot of churches to attend. However, if we pray about the different invites, God will lead us to the right place.

A pastor's word should not only give us comfort, but an understanding of what God command of us. Walk in obedience to the word of God. God's tools work wonderfully, as long as they are used the way God intends for them to be. The misuse of God's tools will not prosper us at all.

Simply ask Him, "Which church should I attend?" God will answer us. If we are not at the point where we can hear God, don't worry. He will still provide an answer to us by other means. Do not fret about it. We will know when it's God. He will even confirm his answer by two or three witnesses.

Remember that Jesus died, so that we could be set free, and have eternal life. To be set free implies that someone was held captive (in bondage). Instead of us (you or I) being held captive or in bondage, He gave His life as a ransom (a replacement) for us. If we have any conscience, we would not want someone to give their life in vain for us to live a bad life. I encourage you to repent to Jesus for living a distasteful or sinful life, which makes what He did (dying) on Calvary's Cross seem unworthy. Repent daily, even if you did no sin in your opinion. Jesus will honor you for it. He is also just in all his ways, even when He gives us favor. God told me that favor is for His children. This lets me know that grace and mercy is for us all. Just try Him!

BACK OF BOOK COVER

People talk about problems all the time, but don't offer real solutions. The author of "Living Single the Right Way" gives you testimonial solutions, biblical principles and sound reasoning to familiar issues, involving single individuals.

As you read, you may recognize the problems in your life or others around you. This book is not designed to tear down anyone, with the issues discussed inside. However, the application of what's inside offers to help progressively transform the individual's mind-set.

Learn how to successfully bring a needed change to your circumstance. Don't ignore or focus only on the problems. Recognize them, and get them fixed!

There is no need for solutions if there are no problems!!! Read this book, and help someone's life.

About The Author

Betty Gibbs is a woman of God who believes in living not just a single's life the right way, but her everyday Christian life as well. She loves helping people, and applying biblical principles to bring empowerment and inspiration to others. Let the wisdom God gives her illuminate your understanding, for a progressive change in your life.

www.ingramcontent.com/pod-product-compliance
Lightning Source LLC
Chambersburg PA
CBHW022121050726
47591CB00002B/876